Contents

Introduction 3

Tidings of Joy From Our Creator 5
(Isaiah 64:1-9; 1 Corinthians 1:3-9; Mark 13:24-37)

Tidings of Comfort, Hope, and Joy 15
(Isaiah 40:1-11; 2 Peter 3:8-15a; Mark 1:1-8)

Tidings of Joy, No Matter What 23
(Isaiah 61:1-4, 8-11; 1 Thessalonians 5:16-24; John 1:6-8, 19-28)

Tidings of Joy in Knowing God 30
(2 Samuel 7:1-11, 16; Luke 1:26-38; Romans 16:25-27)

Tidings of Joy—The Light Is Here! 38
(Isaiah 9:2-7; Titus 2:11-14; Luke 2:1-20)

Meet the Writer 48

Cover photo: Detail of *Adoration of the Magi*, by Sandro Botticello; National Gallery of Art.

Introduction

What an exciting time to be alive! We are just a few days away from a new century and a new millennium. People are fascinated with the idea of completing the second century since Christ's birth. Concern over the possible end of the world is mounting. The news seems filled with worries and evil portents for our world.

Consequently, this year, more than any year we might recall, we need to totally experience the joy of the Advent season. Yes, joy. Deep down abiding joy. I do not mean mere happiness. Happiness is often dependent on circumstances outside us. But joy—deep joy—is not dependent on what happens around us. If we take our focus off external circumstances, we can always find internal joy.

Two thousand years ago a teenage mother had to deliver her child in an animal stall in a strange city, without the aid of a midwife, without the encouragement of her family. That night Mary had plenty to complain about. However, shepherds came to see the child, confirming that this was indeed a special child. The Scriptures tell us she "treasured all these words and pondered them in her heart" (Luke 2:19). Mary chose to ponder the things that brought her great joy from God.

We can likewise make an intentional choice to ponder those things that bring us joy here and now. We have plenty to worry us on any given day. We know, however, that Christ has come and Christ will come again. When he returns, will you be sorrowing and worrying about what is happening around you? Instead, you could be rejoicing in knowing God has kept his promise to the world.

The Advent season is about the joy that comes when we realize that God's grace and mercy, first evidenced in the innocence of a baby boy, stretches down the centuries to encompass our lives. The baby Jesus came for each of us. The man Jesus died for each of us and showed us the way to life eternal. Nothing else will or can happen on this earth that compares with those eternal truths.

Isaiah knew about such grace and mercy; and he, too, lived in difficult times. His prophecies bring us hope that can fill our hearts to overflowing. Luke and Paul wrote about grace and hope and comfort in the midst of such times. A witness like theirs can bring a deep abiding joy to the world around us. Joy in the midst of troubles is what we all truly need in times of crisis. Your abiding joy will speak to the hearts of those around you even if you never speak a word.

I hope that as you prayerfully reflect on the lectionary readings during this advent season, God will fill your heart anew with tidings of comfort and joy and peace and promise of a future—in Christ—filled with God's grace. Christ has come. Christ has risen. Christ will come again!

Tidings of Joy From Our Creator

Scriptures for Advent:
The First Sunday
Isaiah 64:1-9
1 Corinthians 1:3-9
Mark 13:24-37

The lectionary passages for the first Sunday in Advent discuss ways to find joy in our relationship with God. Isaiah describes God as the potter who forms us (the clay) in the ways that please him. Sometimes, when we find ourselves in the midst of painful experiences in our lives, we may not like the way God has formed us. Perhaps we wish we could not get sick or did not have to die. To find God's tidings of joy in Advent is to discover God's redeeming grace even while experiencing such crises.

Paul's warnings to the Corinthian church, though written about two thousand years ago, are still valuable. Don't we, too, struggle with remaining "blameless" each day of our lives? During Advent, we can seek to reassure ourselves and others of the joy of God's love and grace toward us—even though we all are sinners to some extent.

The verses from Mark remind us that as we remember how exciting it must have been when the Messiah was about to be born, we also can look forward with joy and hope for the return of Jesus Christ.

Let us explore what the tidings of joy from our Creator found in these passages can mean to each of us during this Advent season.

TIDINGS FROM THE POTTER TO THE CLAY
Isaiah 64:1-9

Isaiah is one of the most significant of the Old Testament books. Isaiah spoke prophetically to Judah during the critical years of Assyrian expansion, when the Northern Kingdom, Israel, was destroyed. He used names for God that denote power, such as Holy

One and the Judge. Isaiah also presented a clear vision of the Messiah as a servant. His book includes powerful visions of history's end as well.

The Book of Isaiah is often studied by dividing it into two books because the style of message and writing changes after Chapter 40. Many scholars note that the first part of Isaiah (1–39) is filled with visions of judgment interspersed with glimmers of hope for a better day coming to God's people. The second part (40–66) has an exultant tone, looking toward restoration of God's people to Palestine. Together, the two sections of Isaiah present a moving vision of the assured joy and hope of God's people whose times are entirely in God's hands.

God's people are still living in Judah when the Book of Isaiah opens. By the time the last verses are written, the Exile is nearly over. Therefore, when Isaiah uses the word *comfort* in Chapter 40, he means that the people can take comfort for the Exile is nearly over. Hold on, he says, God's redemption is near. Perhaps, as we enter the last Advent season before the new millennium begins, we can look for a similar comfort from God with a fresh, vital expectancy not unlike that when a special baby is about to be born into our family.

A friend of mine makes pottery—not for a living but for the joy of it. Most of us who know her have a piece of pottery that has come directly from her hands. Some are large pieces—vases that hold a wide array of flowers. My gift to remember her by is a communion chalice. It is the blue of a summer sky with delicate lines of gray as accent. Whenever I lift it before the congregation to bless the elements, I think of her loving hands gently forming simple earth into a useful vessel of beauty. And I cannot help but smile.

Isaiah 64:8 reminds us that, in life, God is the potter and we are only the clay—the raw materials. This verse can be comforting to all of us, because it reminds us that since you and I are God-created raw materials, we have what we need to do whatever is required of us.

Maybe that is why Jesus came as a vulnerable baby. Babies are definitely not in control of their life. Nor are we adults, no matter how sophisticated our culture becomes.

In Isaiah 64:1, the writer is begging God to do exactly what God eventually did when Jesus came— to "tear open the heavens and come down, \ so that the mountains would quake at your presence." Most of us have probably prayed a similar prayer at one time or another.

> *Doesn't it seem at times that the world has become so bad that only God could make sense out of it?*

Doesn't it seem at times that the world has become so bad that only God could make sense out of it? Good people seem to get hurt when they stand for what is right. Conversely, people who do bad things often appear to never have trouble.

A friend of mine named John has a storefront ministry on the streets of a large metropolitan city. Some time ago, he called to ask for prayer for his ministry because a large gang had just come to town. One gang member, named Rick, had wandered into the mission one night about midnight. Rick was "high" on amphetamines. His dark brown eyes looked wild. His normally golden brown skin was pale and lusterless. His breath-ing was shallow. John knew the boy was in danger of dying from an overdose, so John closed the storefront and hurriedly took the boy to an emergency room.

After several hours, Rick was stabilized. During Rick's recovery, John stayed most of the days at the hospital with him, only leaving to serve at the storefront ministry at night. Then John took Rick home for a few days to recuperate. Rick had no family or home other than the streets. After a few days at John's house, however, Rick disappeared once again into the anonymity of the streets. As days went by without hearing from Rick, John became depressed to think that Rick had returned to the gang.

Several weeks later, however, Rick came to the mission near midnight once again. There were two other boys with Rick, attired in gang apparel. Both were struggling to breathe just like Rick had been several weeks earlier. John moved toward Rick to see if he, too, was high on drugs. He appeared to be sober.

"These guys need help, John. I told them how you helped me." John was taken aback because he had assumed Rick had fallen back into his old ways. "I even told them about your Jesus. They probably don't believe it any more than I did. Maybe some time they will."

John locked the door to the mission, helped the boys into his car, and once again headed toward the emergency room.

the next two years, the ould repeat itself over and gain. Not all the boys got su... htened out. Some of them died. In fact, John never saw or heard from the majority of them again. But Rick kept bringing them.

Once Rick joined John as he spoke at a fundraiser for the mission. When Rick told his story, John's missionary heart was full. It seemed worth all the sacrifice that John had made for this ministry just to see Rick's progress. Word was getting around the city about how to get out of the slavery of gangs and drugs.

Last Christmas Eve, however, John was on duty late at the mission. Rick appeared at the door of the mission, holding a stumbling gang member. As John opened the door, a car slowed down nearby. Before John realized what was happening, a gun appeared through the open window of the car.

"Merry Christmas, Rick! Here's what we do to guys who take members from us!"

Shots rang out. Rick fell into John's arms, his eyes glazed with death. In a moment like that, while John watched the life ebb from a young man with so much promise, the words of Isaiah made the most sense. Can't you hear John crying out with Isaiah?

"O that you would tear open the heavens and come down, so that the mountains would quake at your presence!"

John was brokenhearted as he opened the door of the mission on the night after Rick's funeral. John asked himself over and over— where is God in all of this? John was angry as he looked at the Christmas tree in the window. It was now obscured from outside view by a piece of plywood placed in the windowpane that had been broken by a stray bullet. John hoped everyone would stay away that night.

Then the door slowly opened, and two young men in gang attire tentatively looked in at John.

John thought about the gun that was now kept nearby in case trouble struck again. Before he could speak to the boys, however, two officers stationed nearby because of the recent shooting grabbed them and pushed them into the mission. One policeman asked, "What are you boys doing here?"

"We came to see Rick's friend," one boy shouted.

John recognized one of the boys. He had been with Rick when he was shot. Quite without realizing it, that boy then spoke words of comfort and joy for John that brought tears to his eyes.

"Rick told me about you. He said you were his friend. Can you help me and my friend, too? We want out." The words of Isaiah were alive in that moment for John as well: "O LORD, you are our Father; we are the clay, and you are our potter" (64:8).

8

Think of a time when your world was shattered by events around you, a time when your faith was tested. What Scripture passages brought comfort and joy?

What times in your life made you wonder if God (as in Isaiah 64:7) had hidden his face from you?

Think of times when you felt that God—in the baby Jesus—had come and torn open the heavens and blessed your life. What contributed to that sense of God's closeness?

TIDINGS OF SALVATION JOY
1 Corinthians 1:3-9

Paul was on his third missionary journey when he wrote his first letter to the troubled church at Corinth. From the contents we can determine that Paul wrote this letter after receiving a verbal report from the respected family of Chloe and that a delegation had come to him asking for his judgment on various specific questions.

The answers Paul gave to the church at Corinth affirm a truth we need to understand in our Christian life today. It is important to realize that our own struggle for a vital faith may be a long one. We should not become discouraged if our journey seems long.

Corinth was a city set in a favor-able spot for trade and sporting events. The fledgling church was surrounded by theaters; areas for Olympic-style athletic competition; and temples, shrines, and altars to various gods and goddesses. Many of the taverns in the city had underground cisterns provided by the city to keep the drinks cool. Even Christians sometimes frequented the temples as they might go to a good steakhouse now. The food there often included meat that had been previously sacrificed to idols.

In addition, people who had come to Corinth to trade their wares brought their cultural influences with them. As Paul introduced the diverse congregation to Jesus Christ, he knew it would not be easy for them to work well in unity.

Isn't this a lot like today? The church is made up of many types of people who come to church with different backgrounds and beliefs. We need to constantly remember that what ties us together is belief in Christ and a desire to become his disciples.

In these verses from First Corinthians, Paul celebrates the grace of God that he hopes is reflected in the Corinthians' speech and actions. He begins with the typical Pauline greeting. He extends grace and peace while recognizing both God and Christ. This recognition affirms that this epistle is a letter to a church.

TIDINGS OF JOY FROM OUR CREATOR

be helpful to remember
are reading someone else's
ike any letter that is written
in response to other correspondence, the writer answers specific questions. We do not have the letter that was written to Paul, nor notes taken when the delegation came to ask him to rule on specific issues. We need to look "between the lines" to try to determine what the questions were so we can know how these answers might be applied.

Paul affirms the faith of those to whom he is writing the letter. He also seems to be reminding the Corinthians who they are—and who God is—and how they are related to God. They are, first of all, believers who "in every way . . . have been enriched by [God]" (1:5). As we move into the Advent season, let us reflect on some ways in which God has also "enriched" our lives.

One way in which God enriches my life comes to mind. Each year as the retail stores begin to introduce Christmas gift items and decorations earlier and earlier, I find myself getting dismayed. This year, however, I decided instead to thank God for bringing the secular world around so well to hear the message of Christ. Sure, a lot of folks just think of the material things. However, along with that, each year the President lights a huge Christmas tree in our nation's capitol; and all over our land colored lights dot the landscape, celebrating this season.

We who understand the full significance of Christ's birth, death, and resurrection might feel badly that these observances sometimes appear to be shallow actions. However, our focus could change when we read Paul's word to Christians who were approaching their faith in a similarly shallow manner.

Perhaps we might try to simply breathe a word of thankfulness at those moments when the world briefly pauses because once, two thousand years ago, a tiny infant made his incarnational appearance in a rude stable in Bethlehem. Along with that prayer of thankfulness, we could celebrate that event to the best of our ability, hoping that other persons will witness the depth of our beliefs and receive the tidings of salvation joy.

Verse 8 reminds us that we shall be strengthened so as to become blameless on the day of our Lord Jesus Christ. Blameless—that sounds impressive, because I know full well that very few moments in my life have been truly "blameless." However, as we look for the joys in this Advent season, one of them surely can be to begin to understand just what being "blameless" can mean.

Think of a time when you were a child and did something wrong. Did you "get away with it"? In other words, did your parents either never find out or, when they did, grant you grace as long as you did not repeat the behavior? If the latter was the case, did you become "blameless" as a result? You still were guilty, but your acts had just been covered with "grace."

Most children (and adults as well) are acquainted enough with life to know when they are doing wrong. We do not have to live very long before we realize being truly "blameless" for us would definitely take divine intervention.

Paul was telling the Corinthians that God has sent that divine intervention. The little baby in the manger grew to be a wise and blameless man who taught us how to live in the best way. Then he died, was resurrected, and showed us how to become blameless in God's eyes. For it is only when we realize we are only human beings on a journey to become the best that God wants us to be that we can know what it means to be "blameless."

Being blameless does not seem to mean to God that we have never sinned. No, it means we have been forgiven. During Advent we expectantly remember the birth of the only one whose grace could make us truly "blameless," no matter what sins we commit.

We can look at 1 Corinthians 1:9 to find out how this happens:

"God is faithful; by him you were called into the fellowship of his Son, Jesus Christ our Lord." That is a powerful reminder of who God is and who we are in relation to God. Only God through Christ can make us "blameless on the day of our Lord." What wonderful tidings of salvation joy!

> *Only God through Christ can make us "blameless on the day of our Lord."*

What does being "blameless," in light of Paul's greeting, mean in your daily life?

What ways do we Christians demonstrate to the world around us that we understand that it is God's grace and Christ's gift to become "blameless"?

What does it mean to be "called into the fellowship of [God's] Son, Jesus Christ our Lord"? In what ways have you experienced that call upon your life? What response could you make to that calling during this Advent season?

TIDINGS OF JOYFUL WAITING
Mark 13:24-37

Oftentimes Christians interpret the Advent season as the time when we remember how it is to wait for the birth of a special baby. We light Advent candles and talk about the coming of that baby. Some celebrations include the baking of a birthday cake for Jesus, lighting the candles during a Christmas program, and sharing presents to remember the gifts that the wise men brought to Jesus. While such observances are appropriate for Advent, if that is all we do during this season, we are missing some of the most powerful Scripture messages related to the season.

Our lectionary reading from Mark is colorfully filled with portent of the final days of earth, the return of Christ, and Christ's reign on earth. In these verses we can hear the prophetic voice of God as Mark carefully describes the ways in which we should be constantly watchful while we are waiting for Christ's return.

It is perhaps best to look at these verses in the context of the rest of Chapter 13. This chapter reports more direct statements by Jesus than any other chapter in the Book of Mark. It is as though Mark wanted to report Jesus' words verbatim in order to make sure he got them right.

The lesson of the fig tree (13:28-31), presented amidst discussion about events expected when Christ comes again, is filled with promises and hopefulness. The people of Mark's time would have understood this parable better than we do. They knew what fig trees look like and how fragile the fruit is. When a tree was filled with leaves, they knew that summer was near because the fig tree could not survive in any other season. Jesus wanted them to know that when these signs and wonders had occurred, he would be "near, at the very gates."

Can we apply these words to the events of today? It seems we can look at the frightening changes in the world around us with joy if we realize that everything is in God's hands. As a matter of fact, all the important things in life—birth, death, sickness, wealth—are always in God's hands. When we face the uncertainties of life, we are forced to face that fact. We can celebrate because there are no better hands in which to rest our lives.

It would be helpful to keep in mind that any events in the world that make us wonder if the end is near—even if they seem as clear a sign as the leaves bursting out on a fig tree—are not to be feared. Jesus has promised that he is near during the worst of times—"even at the gates," ready to come. Fear and sadness should fly away when we focus with joy upon the coming of Christ. Verse 30 is a puzzling statement: "This generation will not pass away until all these things have taken place." Since that generation is long gone, what could Jesus have meant? Scholars are not clear. One meaning for "generation" is "the current generation" or "generation" might mean "a family or a national line." Since the Jewish nation was about to be scattered, the words in verse 30 proved to be a comforting promise from Jesus. He wanted them to remember that though they were dispersed, they would be in God's grace until Christ comes to redeem them.

If one uses the meaning "current generation," however, then perhaps Jesus was making his message relevant to any generation currently alive. Jesus could have been stressing that no one knows the hour of his return; therefore, each generation should assume that their own generation might not pass away before Christ's return. There certainly can be joy in living out our lives in this kind of heightened expectancy.

Jesus reminds us also to be alert (13:32-37). We might ask what we are supposed to be alert about. One meaning is that we should be careful to be alert so that we do not let in the things that sapped the vitality of the religion of Israel.

Perhaps you are wondering why these verses prophesying about Christ's return are included in the Advent lectionary readings. It is because we remember two things during the Advent season. First, we recall the happy expectancy that the birth of Jesus brought. His birth was an outward sign of the incarnation of God in human flesh. The other equally important part of Advent is to think expectantly about and wait joyfully for the return of Christ.

These verses in Mark describe a great and terrible day when "the sun will be darkened" and the moon "will not give its light." "Stars will be falling from heaven, and the powers in the heavens will be shaken" (13:24-25). And there, in the midst of a terrifying scenario, Christ will come in the clouds with even greater power and glory. Some view these events with fear and trembling. Our fears should be calmed when we read verse 27, however: "Then he will send out the angels, and gather his elect from the four winds, from the ends of the earth to the ends of heaven." That will be a glorious day indeed! What a wonderful reason to be joyful while we wait!

What does it mean to be watchful—to keep awake—in light of these verses from Mark?

TIDINGS OF JOY FROM OUR CREATOR

13

In what ways can you demonstrate your joy in that watchfulness in your Advent activities this year?

Reread Mark 13:26-27. Visualize the scene described there. What do you see the people on the ground doing as Christ is coming in the clouds? What do you imagine you will be doing if he comes while you walk this earth?

CONCLUSION

Our lectionary passages from Isaiah, First Corinthians, and Mark all share a common thread of deep abiding joy while waiting. Happiness and joy are quite different. The people of Isaiah's time understood that well. While we are in bondage, happiness may elude us. However, we can still feel joy in God's presence and the promise of hope.

The diverse people in the Corinthian church were much like our diverse congregations today. Some folks actually dread the Advent season, because of bad experiences in their past. Those folks will find little joy in Advent again until they find a way to move their focus to the simplest details of Advent. Christ has come. Christ is risen. Christ will come again!

Mark reminds us of promises that will enable us to focus on this deep joy, if we will heed them. Mark also points out that our hearts can rejoice when the signs of Christ's return are all around us. When we see these signs, as clearly as we may see leaves appearing on a tree, we can smile, knowing Christ is at the gates.

My daughter, Beth, then six years old, called me aside one Christmas to tell me she had figured out "how Jesus gets people into heaven." "Jesus helps them!" she proudly told me. I asked her how Jesus did that. She looked at me with a bit of a frown, rather disgusted that I had not figured this out before myself. "Oh, Mom, he just reaches down and lifts us up to heaven with him." I was stunned.

There is the gospel, the tidings of joy from our Creator, in a sentence. Why not let Jesus lift you up this Advent season. Keep your eyes open, the Scriptures tell us. Jesus Christ is coming again. Watch and wait with joy.

Tidings of Comfort, Hope, and Joy

Scriptures for Advent: The Second Sunday

Isaiah 40:1-11
2 Peter 3:8-15a
Mark 1:1-8

The lectionary readings for the second Sunday of Advent from Isaiah, Second Peter, and Mark call us to live a holy and righteous life. Though this kind of life pleases God and draws us closer to God, the underlying reason we are called to this kind of life is that it is the best way to find ourselves filled with the joy of the Lord.

As we read these passages, let us consider what it means to live in a holy and righteous way. Think about the different ways God calls us to serve. Some are called to be messengers, like John the Baptist, to bring news of someone else who is coming. Others are called to bring the message directly like Jesus did.

Consider also what aspects of the passages might help you know how to live the holy life in the most joyful way. Can you sense the comfort, hope, and joy that living such a life—even in the midst of difficulty—can bring?

One sure way to experience joy in life is to observe small children. If trouble comes on the scene, they respond to it and go on their way. A child's joy is infectious. Catch that joy. Share it and watch it multiply!

TIDINGS OF COMFORT THAT BRING JOY
Isaiah 40:1-11

While my husband and I were ministering in a high security penitentiary, I became acquainted with a young man I shall refer to as Todd. Todd had been convicted of stealing a car at age nineteen. He had been ready to start his second year of college in the fall but got a little high one night and went along with a group of college students who wound up stealing a car. Unfortunately, one of the students pulled a gun when a policeman stopped them; and the policeman was injured. Todd's part in the crime gained him a five-year sentence.

When I met Todd, he was about to be released after serving 3½ years. Like many penitentiary residents, he was rather concerned about getting out. Where would he go? What could he do? His family had abandoned him, and his scholarships had been given to others. Todd was feeling pretty bad about himself and what the future might hold for a convicted felon.

I visited Todd the night before he was to be released. As we read Isaiah 40 together, some new possibilities began to open up in Todd's mind. Todd was amazed that God comforted his people after they did all those bad things. He wanted to know why he did not feel God's comfort much right at that moment. He had never lived on his own before, having moved from home to college dorm to penitentiary. We prayed for Todd to find that comfort and strength.

Following our prayer, Todd said he liked verse 11 because he hoped God would help him through the next few days. Isaiah's words seemed to come alive for Todd while he held the Bible in his hands as we talked. I tried to encourage Todd, by reminding him that these verses were written to comfort God's own disobedient people, not some group of perfect saints. I hoped what I was saying would help. I knew that most young prisoners his age who are released wind up back in the penitentiary fairly quickly. The odds were against Todd making it on the outside without God's grace. I reminded him that he had served his term, just like God's people had, and that his life was still ahead of him.

Todd, like a lot of us, needed to be comforted. Many times life just does not work out the way we had planned.

> *Many times life just does not work out the way we had planned.*

Note that Isaiah's words were not just meant to comfort the people of his time (40:3-5). Isaiah tells of a messenger who will come to prepare the way for the Lord. Mark 1:1-8 identifies John the Baptist as this voice crying out in the wilderness.

Verses 6-11 are sheer poetry. Read them aloud. Notice how the words paint lovely pictures that help us understand what God is saying.

Verse 6 describes people as being like grass and no more constant than the flowers. Can you imagine a field of flowers blowing in a gentle breeze? Flowers are beautiful creations. Wherever they bloom, they bless us with color and, often, fragrance. But all too soon, flowers wither and die. Though grass is green and lush for a while, it too eventually withers and dies.

Isaiah compares these useful and lovely (but fleeting) vulnerable things (grass and flowers) to the word of God. His conclusion is simple. "The word of our God will stand forever," though these creations will soon perish.

Isaiah then tells us that this truth is something to shout about. He tells us to get up on top of the highest mountain and to shout "Here is your God!" If you are like me, that idea is not very inviting. I would much rather sit quietly by and hope for the best. Do you suppose that "mountain" could also have other meanings? Maybe quietly sharing your faith with a friend could be like shouting on a mountaintop. Maybe Isaiah wanted us to understand that we

need to share the comfort and joy we have found, not just keep it for ourselves. Often our own comfort and joy increases when we share comfort and joy with others.

But there is more to consider. The comfort of Isaiah's promises must have settled warmly into the soul of God's people who were locked in bondage. It must have been consoling indeed for them to think about the possibility that their bad times would be over and they would be "going home." Surely this kind of comfort filled their hearts with joy and awe at the goodness of God.

For us, the promise of comfort described in Isaiah is even sweeter. Jesus has come as the prophets said he would. The salvation that Jesus' life and death brought is now eternally ours. We can rest in knowing that God's grace is here— a free gift for Jesus' followers.

The Advent season is a time to remember with expectation the birth of the baby Jesus. It is also a time to reflect on what the coming of that tiny baby really has meant to each of us. We can also look forward to when Christ returns. In light of that promise, we need not fear anything that happens in the meantime. We are all in God's capable hands.

Think about a time when you needed comfort. Where did you find it? How would you describe the joy that came with finding comfort in the midst of difficulty?

Remember a time when you were present to bring comfort to someone else. What were the circumstances? How did your actions help?

Think of a time that you shouted about God on a mountaintop or shared the gospel of Christ with someone. Or, describe the joy and comfort you felt when someone shared the hope of the gospel with you in a time of need.

TIDINGS OF PATIENCE AND HOPE
2 Peter 3:8-15a

We sometimes fail to remember that time is a man-made concept. Thus, when we encounter Scripture passages like 2 Peter 3:8, where we are reminded that with the Lord a day is like a thousand years and a thousand years a day, we begin to understand the eternal nature of God. No matter how we describe time, all of us will come to a point in time when our earthly life will end. Not so with God. To define God is to define his eternal nature.

Our lectionary reading from Second Peter contains some of the most hopeful words in the Bible. They remind us that when we

think God is taking too much time in answering our prayers, we can know God tarries because he wants the best for us. What would be the best for us? According to these verses, the best would be to "[lead] lives of holiness and godliness, waiting for and hastening the coming of the day of God" (3:11-12).

> ## *To define God is to define his eternal nature.*

What does a holy and godly life look like? Do you know anyone who is holy and godly in his or her living? Think about what the person does that makes you think he or she is holy and in what ways you would want to be like him or her.

Some folks tell me that they think that living a godly life is too difficult, so they do not even try. That is sad, because according to these verses, the day is coming when there will be a new heaven and a new earth. Who will people this place? It will be the home of righteousness. In other words, it will be full of "holy" folks.

Whenever I think about what holiness is, I think of Wayne who was our pastor at a church we attended before I was called to the full time ministry. Pastor Wayne, and his wife Mary Anne as well, seemed to embody holiness. Both of them seemed to be intentionally trying to do things that might bring praise to God.

I was a lay leader in the church where Wayne was serving his last pastorate after forty-one years in the pulpit. Wayne taught me a lot of things I would use in my ministry later. One thing he said many times was that he thought that Jesus "hung out" with folks a lot. He said if I wanted to become effective in sharing the gospel message, I would have to take the time to "hang out" with people too.

Though life had not been easy for Wayne and Mary Anne, they seemed to accept things as they were with joyful hearts. My first encounter with Pastor Wayne was following an auto accident wherein a good friend's parents had been seriously injured. During the first critical hours, Wayne sat in the waiting room with family and friends, often praying for my friend's parents to survive.

Wayne kept us busy, talking about all kinds of things, keeping us from focusing constantly on the scariness of the day. The hours seemed to fly by as we shared them with Wayne. Wayne brought joy to a room filled with tension and despair.

Whenever a medical attendant came to report on my friend's parents, Wayne quietly moved to my friend's side, ready to help her in whatever way he could. He often went into the intensive care unit to remind my friend's parents of the loving watch that was just outside their curtained windows. Usually the nurses sent a message back with Wayne as to how the couple was doing, and that helped as well.

Mary Anne often prepared food and goodies to share with others in need. The fact that polio had left Mary Anne on walking crutches for most of her adult life did not stop her from serving others.

The most significant way that these dear people demonstrated holiness was in how they greeted you when you came into a room. Somehow, no matter the time of day or night or the circumstances, Pastor Wayne and Mary Anne acted as though they were extremely blessed just because you stopped by.

I remember occasions when I went to visit them in a depressed mood and, quite before I realized it, their infectious joy about life lifted my spirits. They projected a strong feeling of complete acceptance of me that made me feel as if I were in the presence of an all-loving God. Actions that tend to make those around one believe they have encountered the holiness of Christ are the essence of holiness.

TIDINGS OF COMFORT, HOPE, AND JOY

Again and again, when any of us around them despaired because God's answer seemed slow in coming, Wayne would remind us we needed to be patient with God. "Give God time to work it out. God will, " Wayne told us. I found comfort and hope in those words. God was hearing me. God was acting on my behalf. I just had to wait to see it.

> *Actions that tend to make those around one believe they have encountered the holiness of Christ are the essence of holiness.*

Remember a time in your life when you had no choice but to be patient. What helped you wait for the answer?

Perhaps you are waiting for something to be resolved in your life right now. How can these verses, which discuss the patience that God has demonstrated to obtain salvation for us, help you build up your resolve to wait?

TIDINGS OF THE GOOD NEWS
Mark 1:1-8

Our lectionary reading from Mark 1 introduces John the Baptist. John is the messenger whom the prophets prophesied would come. Note that verse 2, which is from Malachi (3:1), says, "I am sending my messenger ahead of you, who will prepare your way." John, God's messenger, came before Jesus and prepared the way for Jesus' ministry.

Verse 3, quoted from Isaiah 40:3, says this messenger shall be "the voice of one crying out in the wilderness." John literally lived in the wilderness, but there is a deeper meaning to this description of God's messenger. The world that John and Jesus were born into had become a spiritual "wilderness," a place where folks had largely turned their faces away from God. John's message, virtually shouted out into the wilderness, was simple: "Repent and change your ways."

Haven't you had days when you felt like the world of today was a spiritual "wilderness"? In the midst of our current wilderness, we need to hear the voice of God's messenger.

20   **TIDINGS OF JOY**

John must have been a fascinating person to know. He was Jesus' cousin. The two men's outward appearances were quite different, however. Yet they both reflected the heart of God to others. One of the greatest joys—and mysteries—of the Christian faith is that so many different kinds of persons are called to serve God.

> # *In the midst of our current wilderness, we need to hear the voice of God's messenger.*

Mark describes John as a man who wore camel's hair clothing (1:6). Anyone who has ever been around camels will confirm that camel's hair smells very bad and that soaking the hair in dirty river water would only make the smell worse. The camel's hair probably would not have helped John socially. However, it would help insulate John from the heat and cold variations found in the wilderness where he lived.

John's food, which included locusts and honey, may not seem desirable to an American taste; but locusts were ritually pure and are still eaten by desert people today.

During this Advent season, let us think about who God chooses for service. In this passage God chooses a person who would openly declare the tidings of good news, with his life as well as his words. John also humbly reminds us that if we are lucky enough to be a part of God's plan, we need to remember that we are not worthy to stoop down and tie the thong of Jesus' sandals. Yet, we like John can share the tidings of the good news.

The good news of Advent distills to this: Long ago in a place called Bethlehem, a poor young maiden gave birth to a son named Jesus whose godly presence was wrapped in humanity in a way that changed the course of the world. Jesus gave us hope. Jesus gave us a focus for the rest of the ages until he comes again. Advent is a time to remember Jesus' birth with joyous expectation. It is a time to reflect on what the coming of the tiny baby really meant to the world. It is a time to look forward to when Christ comes again.

Perhaps you feel incapable of really understanding these mysteries enough to act upon your faith. Let John the Baptist's actions encourage you. When he could not go himself to ask Jesus, John sent his followers to ask Jesus to explain who he was (Matthew 11:2-6). Jesus did not turn this question away. He replied: "Go tell John what I have been doing."

TIDINGS OF COMFORT, HOPE, AND JOY

This Advent season, let us also focus on what Jesus did and is doing in our lives and world today and tell the good news.

As we enter the Advent season, we need to discover who God's messengers are. Who is God's messenger to you? When that person speaks, what responses do you make to his or her message?

How do you define "good news" in terms of the gospel of Christ?

How can you convey the joy that comes with this message?

Think of times in your life when you were called to bring an important message to someone. How did that feel? Where did you find the strength to follow through? Was the message well received?

CONCLUSION

The lectionary passages for the second Sunday of Advent call us to live a holy and righteous life. Though this kind of life pleases God and draws us closer to God, the underlying reason that God calls us to this kind of life is that it is the best way to find ourselves filled with the comfort, hope, and joy of the Lord.

Through Isaiah, God said he would send his messenger. In Mark, John arrives and brings joy to the wilderness in which he lives. We, too, can bring tidings of joy to the wilderness places of our world. Second Peter affirms a way to do that as we seek to live a holy and righteous life.

Jesus came to show us the way to salvation. Some of us are called to be messengers like John the Baptist. All of us are called to be disciples and to share the gospel message with others to the best of our ability. Life is brief, Isaiah writes. Only God is eternal. Knowing that, we can live in joyful expectation that God will do what he has promised.

Tidings of Joy, No Matter What

Scriptures for Advent:
The Third Sunday
Isaiah 61:1-4, 8-11
1 Thessalonians 5:16-24
John 1:6-8, 19-28

The three lectionary readings for the third Sunday in Advent combine to bring a powerful message of redemption and hopefulness. Isaiah 61 speaks of the way in which God acts to redeem us from our sins. John 1 reminds us that Jesus is "the light" who will bring us out of the darkness of our sin. First Thessalonians 5 reports the hope and joy that a redeemed follower of Jesus may find in life.

The Thessalonian verses also remind us that as Christians we need to be intentional in living out and witnessing to our faith. We need to be disciplined if we hope to rejoice always and to pray without ceasing. It does not just happen. We must plan for our lives to be enriched by these attributes inherent only in living a life in the grace of God. When we are, we will receive tidings of joy, no matter what.

TIDINGS OF JOY IN REDEMPTION
Isaiah 61:1-4, 8-11

Advent is a season based on expectancy. We remember the time when the world was waiting for the Messiah to be born. Those who knew the prophecies thought they had figured out God's plans well. They must have been somewhat surprised when Jesus came as a baby. A helpless baby was probably the last thing wanted by those who were praying that the Messiah would come quickly to solve their immediate problems. They knew the baby would have to grow up to have any power. Growing up takes time.

Our lectionary reading from Isaiah (61:1-4, 8-11) reminds us, however, that during times when we are waiting, we can look to God for help. God promises "to bind up the brokenhearted." One of the hardest times to rejoice is when we have lost someone close to us. Yet Isaiah 61:3 says God will "give [us] a garland instead of ashes," "the oil of gladness instead of mourning." Only God can provide deep joy in the midst of deep pain because only God can offer us eternal hope through Jesus Christ.

Often it seems that God's waiting people are not treated fairly. Isaiah 61:8-11, however, reminds us that God "love[s] justice" and "hate[s] robbery and wrongdoing." One of the temptations we all face when others do unjust or bad things to us is to want to do bad things in return. Isaiah says that God will not welcome our acting in unjust ways any more than the folks who have treated us wrongly.

Verse 8b is a verse of comfort for us while we wait, for the Lord who loves justice will give his people their "recompense"; and God will make an everlasting covenant with his people. The details of God's blessings to come are listed in Isaiah 61:9-11. When we are feeling down, we can read these verses and be reminded of God's eternal promises. Remember, only God can make truly eternal promises that are always in effect.

Can you visualize the garden described in verse 11? Can you see a garden where shoots are springing up? How lovely would our world

> ## *Only God can make truly eternal promises that are always in effect.*

be if righteousness and praise were "springing up" in the same way in the world around us?

In choosing the words *spring up*, Isaiah denotes prophetic promise to a people tired of injustice and wars. Life is no different now than it was then. We are just as ready for "shoots of righteousness" to spring up. We cannot make others act in righteousness, but we can decide to be shoots of righteousness ourselves.

The tiny baby in the manger grew into a truly righteous man. Jesus showed us the way, but his example is not easy to follow. He asks a lot of us. Perhaps such actions are so powerful because it is so difficult to always act in righteous ways. The Advent season is a time to demonstrate our belief in God. Can you think of ways to do that during this Advent season?

In the sixth chapter of Micah, a lengthy section discusses what God requires of us as his people. Micah

24   **TIDINGS OF JOY**

asks if what God wants are burnt offerings or "thousands of rams" or "ten thousands of rivers of oil" or "our firstborn" for our transgressions (6:6-7). The answer to Micah is simple and clear: "Do justice, . . . love kindness, and . . . walk humbly with your God" (6:8).

No doubt God loves justice, as Isaiah confirms. It would follow that in order to be God's followers, we must love justice too. God hates robbery and wrongdoing also (61:8). It should fairly fill our hearts to bursting with joy to think that the God of the universe cares about whether we are being treated justly. Isaiah 61:10 tells us to "greatly rejoice in the *Lord*, my whole being shall exult in my God."

Are you rejoicing this Advent season? Are you exulting in the Lord? *Exulting* is a word that implies "joy to the extreme." First Thessalonians 5:17-18 reminds us to "rejoice always" and to "pray without ceasing."

I had a friend who decided to practice this discipline for twenty-four hours. The day began with rainy weather and a flat tire on her car. She lives in the country and teaches at a school in town. Her son had borrowed her cell phone. She had to walk a half mile to find a farmhouse with anyone home so she might call for help and inform her principal she would be late to her first class.

By the time she got to the school, soaking wet from the rain, shoes covered with mud, her first class was over. The principal had been filling in for her but had not found her lesson plan. As she walked in, the principal cheerfully asked how she was doing. Remembering her vow, my friend smiled and said, "I'm OK. No, I'm not just OK, I'm rejoicing over this day!" The principal quickly left the room with a look on his face that suggested he was wondering if the rain had done something to her brain.

My friend told me that the rest of the day was not much better. She found out that when trying to "rejoice always," one needs to "pray without ceasing." I asked her how she felt at the end of the day. "Worn out!" she replied. "I felt like I was in a battle with myself all day."

Isaiah understood we would be battling ourselves. He tells us God has thought about that and has helped us out. "He has covered [us] with the robe of righteousness" (61:10b); God has redeemed us. The only one who can cover our sins with righteousness is God. Isaiah describes this beautiful robe as a bridegroom's garland and as jewels for a bride.

Note how in 61:3, Isaiah says we shall be given a "garland instead of ashes, the oil of gladness instead of mourning." Thus God promises that our sins that would alienate us from God and lead to death (ashes) will instead result in God crowning us with a garland of victory.

Advent is a time to remember that our salvation, our redemption, has been won by Jesus. No matter what befalls us, we can rest on that. And in our joy, we need also to continually work for justice wherever we encounter injustice. Often we do not have to look far to see injustice, even in this free country of ours. Though we cannot always eradicate the source of injustice, we can bless the situation with kindness.

Kindness is the oil in the engine of life that makes life worth living. One of the reasons that simple kindness is so powerful in cases of injustice is that victims often have found little kindness in their plight. One kind act can bless a person for a long time. It can energize a person to believe that, though he or she has been unjustly treated, kindness still exists.

A kindness given often fills both giver and receiver with joy. This Advent season, let us look for ways to be kind. Such acts can offer tidings of joy, no matter what the situation.

Have you ever found yourself in a role where you could help either physically or spiritually free others? What did you do?

Would these verses from Isaiah bring comfort in a situation where someone else (or yourself) was in bondage? In what ways might they help?

Describe a time when you or someone you know felt you were in bondage and desperately wanted to be free. Can you recall the joy that freedom from that bondage brought? (Bondage can be anything that keeps you from being or doing all that you are called to be or do.)

In what ways is it comforting to you to think about being "a people whom the *Lord* has blessed" with redemption?

Have you ever tried to "rejoice always" or to "pray without ceasing"? What was the result?

How might you use this passage from Isaiah to bring comfort to someone in mourning?

> ## *Kindness is the oil in the engine of life that makes life worth living.*

TIDINGS OF JOY TO THE FAITHFUL
John 1:6-8, 19-28

Our lectionary reading from John (1:6-8, 19-28) is quite similar to Lesson Two's reading from the Book of Mark. The verses from Mark (1:1-8) refer to the prophecy from Isaiah 40 about the coming of John the Baptist and describe John's lifestyle and appearance. Our reading for this lesson reflects the writer of the Gospel of John's tendency to interpret events rather than just to report them.

The Gospel of Mark uses Isaiah 40:3 to give further credibility to both John the Baptist and Jesus. This lesson's reading moves quickly into a metaphor to explain the relationship between John and Jesus, as well as the differences in their calling. A metaphor goes beyond just comparing one thing to another. In a metaphor, one thing is the other thing.

According to John 1:6-8, John the Baptist was not "the light"; but he came to bear witness to it. Jesus was "the light." By referring to Jesus as "the light," the Gospel writer sends a strong signal to his readers. God is the one who spoke "light" into existence. Only our creator God could do that, and only God could send "the light"— Jesus.

Light and darkness are used as metaphors for God and evil or good and evil throughout the Bible. Psalm 27:1 says: "The LORD is my light and my salvation." Isaiah 9:2 reminds God's people: "The people who walked in darkness have seen a great light." Isaiah did not mean "light" literally but as a metaphor for the power of God entering people's lives and bringing truth. In Matthew 5:14, Jesus tells his disciples: "You are the light of the world." His words imply that Jesus was passing on this metaphor and the power it represented to his followers, including present-day believers.

But how can Jesus be "the light"? Jesus is the one who can enter our life so completely that there is no room left for darkness. What a source of joy for the faithful!

Note that our lectionary reading skips John 1:9-18. You might want to take time to read those verses since they further confirm the tie between God the Creator and Jesus "the light."

The writer of John makes clear in verses 19-28 that John the Baptist was not "the light," the Messiah. One day while John was baptizing repentant persons in the Jordan River, some priests and Levites came to ask him questions. They were curious about who John was.

TIDINGS OF JOY, NO MATTER WHAT

Verse 24 tells us that the Pharisees had sent these people to John, so we need not be surprised at the questions they asked of him. They asked John if he was Elijah or the prophet. John answered no and by his answer (1:23) confirmed that he was part of the fulfillment of the prophecies about the Messiah found in Isaiah.

John left it to his questioners, and to us, to decide for ourselves who he was as we realize more fully the power that God gives to those who accept his will. Like Mary, the mother of Jesus, John the Baptist lived out the role of a bondservant to God. He could have refused to continue to serve God at any time, as we can; but instead John decided to remain faithful to death, even death as a martyr. Can we be as faithful? Can we proclaim tidings of joy, no matter what?

How has your faithfulness to Jesus Christ brought light into your life?

What aspect of John the Baptist's actions in this passage might help you be able to remain faithful?

TIDINGS OF JOY—ANYWAY!
1 Thessalonians 5:16-24

If ever a group of verses reflected the true spirit of Advent and Christmas, it is 1 Thessalonians 5:16-24. Imagine how the world might be if we were all to:

(verse 16) Rejoice always
(verse 17) Pray without ceasing
(verse 18) Give thanks in all circumstances
(verse 19) Not quench the Spirit
(verse 20) Not despise the words of prophets
(verse 21a) Test everything
(verse 21b) Hold fast to what is good
(verse 22) Abstain from every form of evil
(verse 23a) Let God sanctify you
(verse 23b) Keep your spirit, soul, and body blameless until Christ comes
(verse 24) Know God is faithful

Most of us look at the above list and say, "impossible," probably because of the words *always, not, every,* and *blameless.* We all know we are sinners and, as sinners, we can fail to "always" do everything we should.

According to these words from First Thessalonians, Christians need to witness by their daily lives as well as their actions. At times it is hard to "hold fast to what is good" when everyone around you mocks you for trying to do so. And yet, following the admonition to hold fast to what is good has another side: "Abstain from every form of evil." If we were able to abstain from evil, we would at the same time hold fast to what is good.

Nor is it an easy thing to keep our spirit, soul, and body blameless until Christ comes again. First Thessalonians tells us, however, that it is possible through the grace of God to do just that. This Advent season, let us set our goals high. If we set them high and do not quite make it, we shall be further along in our spiritual journey than if we set them low. And, in the process, we shall be allowing God to sanctify us—make us holier and more like Jesus Christ. And we will receive tidings of joy—anyway.

What effect might living by the words of this passage have on your daily life?

How has the grace of God provided support for your spiritual journey?

CONCLUSION

This Advent season, fill your heart with joy as you think about God wrapping himself in human flesh and coming to walk among us and show us the way to God. Is that hard to do in a world like ours? Maybe it would help to imagine that you are wrapping "the robe of righteousness" around you as Isaiah described it.

Certainly John the Baptist understood what it meant to rejoice in all things. John seemed to know that God was the real source of the light and power in his life. As a result, John always gave the glory to God.

I once met a man with a terribly deformed face. For years he stayed away from people, fearing their response to his deformity. Then one day he decided to just go out and live the life described in our First Thessalonians reading. When people pulled back from him or refused to look at his face, he would simply say, "I'm sorry that you will never get to know me, because you are missing one of God's own sons!" Then he would extend his hand to them. Not everyone took it. Those of us who did were blessed with a person who understands fully what it means to spread tidings of joy, no matter what.

Tidings of Joy in Knowing God

Scriptures for Advent:
The Fourth Sunday
2 Samuel 7:1-11, 16
Luke 1:26-38
Romans 16:25-27

What would it feel like to move through the Advent season with a "right heart"? Perhaps some of our depression and dismay with the shallowness of the Christmas celebrations around us might disappear if we could somehow worry less about others and keep our own hearts "right" with God. In the lectionary passages for the fourth Sunday of Advent, we shall read about some ways to do just that.

In Second Samuel we find that God is looking for leaders with a right heart for God, even if they are not perfect. People like David. People like us, perhaps? In the verses in Luke 1, we hear Mary's humble response to the news that she will give birth to the Messiah. As she ponders what it means to be "blessed," perhaps we might think about how we can be blessings to others in the circumstances in which we live. And, in the verses from Romans, we are called to think deeply about who God is and to praise God. In so doing, we will discover some ways to make our hearts "right" with God.

TIDINGS OF A RIGHT HEART
2 Samuel 7:1-11, 16

The part of Second Samuel from which our lectionary reading comes covers the rule of David over Israel. At this time, there was no temple to house the ark of the covenant; so David decided to build God a permanent physical structure instead of the tent or Tabernacle then in use. But God told David, through the prophet Nathan, that God would build a "house" for David instead. God would make David the father of a "house" or line of kings. In doing so David's "kingdom shall be made sure forever . . . [his] throne shall

30   TIDINGS OF JOY

be established forever" (7:16).

God reminded David, through Nathan, that it was God who brought David "from the pasture, from following the sheep to be prince over my people Israel" (7:8). In this Advent season, we remember that Jesus was of the house and lineage of David. God chose Jesus' family for him. Family lineage was extremely important to God's people. They would have never listened to someone whose lineage was not as the prophets said it would be—from the house of David.

The fact that God chose the house of David to honor in this way has always fascinated me. David was a good person, and he seemed to truly want to serve God. However, on many occasions, David sinned and took his eyes off God's purposes for his life. Perhaps the reason that God did not give up on David was because no matter how many times David failed God, David always came back to God repentant about his sins and wanting to reconcile with God.

God was not looking for perfection in his leaders; he was looking for leaders with a right heart for God. That is encouraging to us. God used and honored David even though he stole a man's wife from him, had the man killed, and only repented after the child he fathered with that woman died. There is hope for all of us who want to serve God but know that we are not perfect.

That is part of the tidings of joy we celebrate this Advent Season. God made us just the way we are and loves us the way we are, especially

> *God made us just the way we are and loves us the way we are.*

when we keep on trying to move back toward a relationship with God.

We have a new grandchild named Caelan (Scottish for "Nicolas"). I arrived at the hospital not long after Caelan was born; and as we all stood gazing at him in the birthing room, we searched for those ways in which he looks like my daughter who is his mother and of course the rest of us. We spent the day in awe of how much he resembles the McQueens. When his other grandparents arrived a little later, they found great joy in noting Caelan's cleft

TIDINGS OF JOY IN KNOWING GOD

chin, which was like his uncle's, and other things about him that they claimed. It was a joyous day of embracing a new member of the family.

As I reached the end of that wonderful day and was thanking God in prayer for the events surrounding Caelan's birth, I wondered if God sometimes has experiences like that with us. The Bible says we are made in God's image. So I hoped God sometimes has reason to look at each of us and smile, saying: "Why, she or he makes me think of my Son Jesus." I hope so. This Advent season, may we make our hearts right so that we can bring God such joy.

The Bible says that David wrote Psalm 51 after his sin with Bathsheba and while he was trying to get back to a proper relationship with God. Wouldn't our hearts be filled with joy if God did, indeed, "create in [us] a clean heart"? How would you respond to the joy of knowing God in this way?

What do you think is significant about Jesus coming from the house and lineage of a king who sinned like David? What does this say about the humanity of Jesus? about our humanity?

TIDINGS OF JOY TO GOD'S SERVANTS
Luke 1:26-38

Note that our lectionary reading from Luke refers to the promise made to David in Second Samuel. The child to be born to Mary will be given "the throne of his ancestor David" (1:32). The promise of an unending "house" made so long ago has been fulfilled: "He will reign over the house of Jacob forever" (1:33). Jesus "will be great, and will be called the Son of the Most High" (1:32). He will bring tidings of joy to all God's servants.

It is significant that the archangel Gabriel is the messenger who comes to tell Mary about the impending birth of the child who will fulfill the promise. Gabriel means "man of God." God has sent one of his own, one of the highest ranking angels, for the task of bearing the most important news in the Bible. The centuries of alienation from God are just about over.

We should not be surprised, then, that Luke reports that Mary was "much perplexed" at Gabriel's greeting: "Greetings, favored one! The Lord is with you" (1:28). Gabriel tried to comfort Mary by saying she need not be afraid "for you have found favor with God" (1:30). Surely Mary's heart must have skipped another beat, however, as Gabriel continued: "You will conceive in your womb and bear a son, and you will name him Jesus" (1:31).

The name *Jesus* may have had great significance to Mary. Perhaps she was aware that *Jeshua* (Hebrew for Jesus) means "He will save." The name had a long history related to the covenant God had made with the Hebrew nation, a history that Mary's people had passed from generation to generation for centuries.

Gabriel did not stop with telling Mary about the name of her child, however. He clearly defined who Jesus would be—the Son of the Most High and the heir to David's throne. He would live forever and have an endless kingdom. Then Gabriel told Mary about another miraculous event—that her relative Elizabeth who was considered to be barren was already pregnant with a special child.

We can almost hear Mary's thoughts: *Me? A teenage girl? I shall be mother of the Messiah?* So her next question makes a lot of sense. "How can this be, since I am a virgin?" (1:34). Christians have been asking this question over the centuries since. No one is certain just how the Holy Spirit "overshadowed" this young woman so that she conceived a child.

This is a faith question because it is impossible to test. In scientific inquiry only repeatable events can be truly studied. Scientists maintain that one can only come to a clear solution for repeatable events. One of the joys of the Advent season, however, can be found when we realize that this event never needs to be repeated. Jesus came, died, and was resurrected. He was just what Gabriel said he would be—a great deliverer—and Jesus will live forever, endlessly serving on the throne of David and saving God's people.

With Mary, as with David in Second Samuel, God was looking for a right heart. Verse 38 tells us that God found just such a heart in Mary, for she humbly reassured Gabriel and God: "Here am I, the servant of the Lord; let it be with me according to your word."

Gabriel left as soon as he heard Mary accept what God was bringing into her body and her life. What God was doing for Mary was a glorious thing—making her the mother of the Messiah. Though this glorious thing was miraculous, it also meant that Mary must be the human being bringing the miracle to pass with her faithfulness. Mary would have to walk through pregnancy and shame and risk losing Joseph, the man she planned to marry. What if he failed to accept God's plan?

Note that the Greek word translated as "servant" in Luke 1:38 is the same used by Paul when he referred to himself as "a servant of

TIDINGS OF JOY IN KNOWING GOD

Christ Jesus" (Romans 1:1; Philippians 1:1). A servant or bondservant is a slave who has been set free by his or her master but who voluntarily returns to serve the former master because of love and loyalty. In effect, the person puts himself or herself in bondage to the former master. The use of this word in Mary's answer to God means God did not force Mary to do his will. God gave Mary the opportunity to accept or refuse his will. Mary accepted.

We are all given the same gracious offer to do God's will in our lives. God wants us to serve him because we choose to. During this

> # God wants us to serve him because we choose to.

Advent season, let's think about whether we could be a bondservant to God—to Jesus. Like Mary, if we accept God's offer of freedom from sin, much will be expected of us. But also, like Mary, there are wonderful rewards in God's kingdom for those who will receive them. It is exciting to think that when we accept God's grace, we become part of the fulfillment of the promise Gabriel gave to Mary—"and of his kingdom there will be no end" (1:33).

Let us not devalue the fact that Mary had a difficult task before her, however. Because the Scriptures only describe a few scenes in Mary's life, we might only think of her in limited ways. We see her kneeling before the angel Gabriel. We think of her holding a sweet newborn baby, seeking asylum in Egypt when that baby's life is threatened, and looking for the young Jesus in the Temple. Or, maybe we picture Mary at the cross or in the upper room waiting for the Spirit to come upon her again. We need to remember, however, that between these limited portrayals Mary lived her life as the mother of Jesus. She nursed and trained and raised the Messiah for us.

No doubt at times Mary knew the scorn of her neighbors. Many of us, when faced with such fearful situations or when having to do a difficult task, would respond negatively. We would complain, hoping to escape the situation. We might blame others and feel victimized by the events in our lives. Might we during this Advent find a way to treasure the circumstances of our lives in our hearts like God's servant Mary (Luke 2:19), instead of letting them get us down.

When have you been able to rejoice in God despite your outward circumstances?

What does the word *servant* mean in your Christian journey?

TIDINGS OF JOY IN KNOWING WHO GOD IS
Romans 16:25-27

Paul did not found the church at Rome; but he wrote to them to introduce himself, probably from Corinth. Our lectionary passage is the concluding verses of the letter, a doxology, a hymn of praise to God. In this doxology, Paul confirms again who God is, who we of the church are, and how we are related to God. God can:

—strengthen us

—become known to Gentiles through prophetic writings

—live eternally

—bring about obedience to faith

—be wise

—operate through Jesus Christ forever.

Paul's words were a significant affirmation for the Gentiles in this early church that God can become known to Gentiles through prophetic writings. For a conservative Jew in the Roman church, however, Paul's affirmation would have been hard to accept. Many Jews believed that God's prophetic writings belonged only to the Jews.

Paul's affirmation of God's eternal nature was also an affirmation that the God of the Jews was the God of the Gentiles. Though this confirmation of who God is was controversial for some of the early Jewish Christians, it was, no doubt, a blessed confirmation to the Gentiles. (And still is an affirmation for us Gentiles today.)

Only God has an eternal nature. On those days when we feel we cannot feel God's presence in our hearts, this affirmation from Paul can help us move closer to God again. We can be sure of God's presence. How can we be sure? Paul says the eternal God will operate through Jesus Christ forever. That means Jesus is eternally near to minister to us. Paul uses strong

> *Jesus is eternally near to minister to us.*

absolute words in this affirmation. *Forever* can have no "qualifier" attached to it in these verses. God is either eternal or God is not. One cannot be a little bit "eternal" in nature.

The Advent season is nearly over now. Christmas day will be here next Saturday. May Paul's doxology help us express the tidings of joy we have in knowing who God is and experiencing God's presence in our hearts this Christmas.

What have you learned about the nature of God from Paul's doxology?

What does it mean to you that we are eternally surrounded by God's presence?

Where has your Advent journey taken you this year?

In what ways have you experienced the coming of the Christ Child in your heart this Christmas?

In what ways have you expanded your expectancy of Christ's coming again?

CONCLUSION

In this lesson we have reflected on the promises made by God in Second Samuel 7 and the humble yet powerful response of Mary to God's pronouncement about her becoming the mother of the Messiah. We have also looked at Paul's doxology to the Roman church. Each of the passages affirms the truths about the nature of God found in the other two.

The Advent season is only rich with the full joy of expectancy to the extent that we understand who it was who came two thousand years ago. He was Emmanuel, God with us. But just what does that mean? In our quest to find the truth about God and Jesus Christ for our own lives, it is encouraging to find passages like these that affirm who Jesus had to be if he were really the Messiah.

When I was a small child, I remember going to a Christmas Eve service. The traditional Nativity pageant was acted out by nervous fourth-graders who wore bathrobes and towels wrapped turban-like on their heads. "Mary" was holding a real wiggling four-month-old baby, and I remember thinking at one point that Jesus was certainly alert and strong for a newborn baby. And big, too.

Over the "manger" was a large star cut out of cardboard and covered with aluminum foil. The pastor pointed to the star and said it was a sign in the Eastern sky that Jesus was coming.

As we drove home that night, I asked Mama which direction was east. In the morning, I was up before dawn, hardly able to wait for everyone to wake up and open presents. But I had something else on my mind too. I wanted to check out whether there was a star in the East that morning.

I stole quietly outside and looked up in the direction Mama had shown me. Sure enough, one star was brighter than all the rest. I was so excited. I could not wait to show it to Mama before the sun obscured it from view. I went scurrying into the house shouting, "There's a star in the East! There's a star in the East!"

Needless to say, the rest of the family were not nearly so thrilled about going out to see the star as I was. But, finally, Mama and my sister dragged themselves from bed and went out with me to look. The star was fading fast as the first rays of sunshine stole across the Christmas morning sky.

Years later, when Christmas came around, I remembered that morning. I woke early and looked out, and sure enough there was one star brighter than the others in the early morning sky. My husband smiled and said, "Mars, probably." That didn't matter. I picked up the phone at 6:00 A.M. (4:00 A.M. on the West Coast where my mother lived).

Mama sleepily answered the phone. "There's a star in the East!" I shouted into the receiver. "Look, there's a star in the East!"

"You nut," my mother laughingly answered. But she got up and looked out the window. "Can't really see it from here, Mary."

"I know," I told her. "Because you can only find it in your heart. Merry Christmas, Mama." "Merry Christmas, Baby, and . . . thanks."

Over the years, we often began our Christmas greetings to one another with "Look, there's a star in the East!" Last year, Mama had gone home to heaven. But I went out on Christmas morning and looked up and hollered to the sky, "Look, there's a star in the East!" And it was there again, in my heart, along with Mama. That's what Advent is all about—remembering who our God is in expectant hope. Christ is coming. Christ has come. Christ will come again. What wonderful tidings of joy!

Tidings of Joy— The Light Is Here!

Scriptures for Christmas:
Isaiah 9:2-7
Titus 2:11-14
Luke 2:1-20

Jesus came to bring the light of hope and joy to the world. One can hear the words of Isaiah 9:2-7 as we think about the Babe in the manger, for the manger of Luke 2:1-20 contained the fulfillment of these prophecies of light coming into the darkness.

It only takes a small amount of light to dispel total darkness. Living in that light sometimes involves sacrifice and doing good works. We do not need to do good works in order to gain salvation, however. Jesus has already done that for us. Titus tells us that once we have received salvation, we are free to live self-controlled lives in the light while we wait for Christ's return.

Are you approaching the manger this Christmas thinking you will only be hearing "the same old story" again? Then come into the light and rejoice. View the manger in a new and fresh light; for Christ has come. Christ has risen. Christ will come again!

TIDINGS OF JOY—THE LIGHT WILL COME
Isaiah 9:2-7

Finding complete darkness on this earth is difficult, for even the tiniest light will break complete darkness. A lighted candle held high on the open plains or in a deep valley can be seen for some distance, probably because it is such a contrast to the darkness that surrounds it.

Once I visited a series of caves in California where a guide led us deep under the ground. First, we each received a miner's hat with a small light. Then we climbed into tiny train-like cars to ride a double rail into the mountain. When we reached a large cavern, we stood in a large circle, marveling at the ancient rock formations around us. Our lights sparkled off the long, slender icicle-like stalagmites and stalagtites.

Then the guide asked, "How many of you have ever been in total darkness?" A few hands went up. "Well, in a few minutes, you will experience one of the few places on this earth that you can be in total darkness. On my cue, will you all turn off your headlamps?"

I was already feeling some claustrophobia about this place, knowing we were over a mile under the mountain. Now the guide was proposing total darkness. I looked around, trying to keep others from noticing I was making sure I remembered how to get out of here if I needed it. Others were looking too. Then the guide gave the cue.

Suddenly we were all surrounded by a level of darkness I had never experienced elsewhere. The cavern, which had been filled with our voices before, fell silent. It was totally dark. I raised my hand directly in front of my face, but I could not see it. Fortunately for the meeker persons like myself, the guide only allowed about two minutes of total darkness before he lit a small cigarette lighter.

What that tiny flickering light did to the totally black room was amazing. The guide was standing in the center of our circle. As he slowly turned around the circle, we got a glimpse of what a small amount of light can bring to even the darkest places on earth. Just that single flame allowed us to see his hands, a bit of his face, and most of the trunk of his body.

"It only takes a slight amount of light to dispel total darkness," the guide said, over and over, as he turned. Then we all breathed easier as he gave the cue to turn on our headlamps again. Having experienced total darkness, the cavern now literally burst into light and beauty. Yet not nearly as much beauty as when on an evening two thousand years ago the Light in the form of a tiny baby came to dispell the darkness forever.

Candlelight services on Christmas Eve are a longstanding tradition. If you have ever participated in such a service, think about the quiet darkness that is gradually dispelled as each person shares the light of an individual candle with a neighbor. Think about how much light is generated by so many persons all contributing their light to that room. Remember how that tiny flame represents the light that came into the world when Christ first allowed himself to be wrapped in fragile human flesh.

The world may have thought that tiny baby had no power. The world was wrong. Isaiah tells us

TIDINGS OF JOY—THE LIGHT IS HERE!

"the rest of the story," which confirms Jesus' real power. "Authority rests upon his shoulders; and he is named Wonderful Counselor, Mighty God, Everlasting Father, Prince of Peace" (9:6b). When we recognze who this tiny infant is, we come to life. We allow the light Jesus Christ brought to shine in our lives—the light that cannot be put out, that dispells the darkness.

As we move through this last Christmas season of the twentieth century, share this light with others. Then those who follow in the coming century will know the joy of its glow in their lives, too.

What does it mean to you that Jesus Christ brought light to the darkness of our world?

How do you find comfort and joy in Isaiah's words as you move through this Christmas season?

TIDINGS THAT GOD IS ALL WE NEED
Titus 2:11-14

The Book of Titus is one of three letters written by Paul to two young men whom he had trained for the ministry. These letters, which include First and Second Timothy as well as Titus, are called the "Pastoral Epistles."

Timothy and Titus were not pastors in the modern day sense of the word. They did not have a particular congregation but rather traveled to churches when problems emerged. In modern times, we might call them "church troubleshooters."

Since Timothy was with Paul on his last missionary journey, these letters may have been written during Paul's imprisonment in Rome. Thus, we can assume that these three letters reflect some of Paul's last words, probably penned about thirty years after Jesus' death. Paul was confined to chains during that imprisonment. Yet he did not let even the chains stop him from teaching the truth.

The church was growing as the gospel message was bringing hope and life to many first-century pagans. The early apostles, including Paul, Peter, Barnabas, John, Apollos, Priscilla, and others, were now old. The church included second- and third-generation believers. The Roman government was about to take an official position against Christianity.

The grace of God has appeared and brought salvation to us all.

Paul reminds us (in verse 11) that it is the grace of God that has appeared and brought salvation to us all, which allows us to grow in personal piety with God despite any present difficulties. We can be filled with confidence and joy in reading Paul's words that once again confirm God has given us all that we need to walk more closely with God.

Do you have difficulty with the word *piety*? Sometimes we focus on false piety or self-righteousness. Paul describes piety in this passage. Piety—living close to God—is accomplished when we "renounce impiety and worldly passions" (2:12). Paul also states we are to "live lives that are self-controlled, upright, and godly, while we wait for the blessed hope and the manifestation of the glory of our great God and Savior, Jesus Christ" (2:12-13).

Before Jesus came, if we wanted to live a godly life, we must know all the laws and try to obey them. Jesus freed us from the necessity of obeying the law, although it is reasonable to expect that those who know and worship Jesus Christ will do good works. We do not need to do good works in order to gain salvation. Rather, good deeds flow out of our love and praise for God through Christ.

Several years ago, I had the privilege of working with a group of street youth from a fairly large metropolitan city. One morning, as I led the youth Sunday School class at our small suburban church, two young girls walked in off the street and joined us. They used raw street language and obviously were not too comfortable in a church setting. I soon discovered that they were hungry. So I sent one of the teens down to the local bakery for doughnuts. They ate like it was their only meal of the day. Probably because it was.

> *Good deeds flow out of our love and praise for God through Christ.*

I contacted the ladies in our church and asked if they could provide food weekly during the youth class. They were delighted, probably not realizing they were signing on for a three-year mission to these youth. As the weeks went by, more street youth joined us. We took them to Christian rock concerts, youth rallies, and nursing homes and walked them through the basic beliefs of the Bible during the weekly Sunday school classes.

As Christmas drew near, I helped them prepare a program for Christmas Eve. They worked hard each week to get ready for the big night, missing very few Sundays (as long as we kept having lots of good food).

The Christmas Eve program was scheduled for 7:00 P.M. My husband, Ken, and I became alarmed when six o'clock came and went and there were no youth present to do their part of the program. We had the whole chancel area set up for their presentation, which was to be the first event.

Finally Ken decided to go looking for the youth in the church van. He found some of them standing on a street corner, some of them at one of the girls' homes drinking beer, and some of them behind the schoolhouse.

Meanwhile, back at the church, we were making plans in case none of them showed up. The organist began to play. The church was packed. When there were no youth in sight at the appointed hour, we rewrote the order of the bulletin and asked the kindergartners to start the evening's program with a song.

One gentleman who had not been in favor of us spending "so much time on those street youth" whispered, "I told you those kids were no good. They won't be here." My heart was racing with anxiety by the time the kindergarten children took their last bow. Then I heard the van driving up beside the church.

We still had a dilemma. We were certain the youth all knew their parts, or had known them as of the previous Sunday. But would they cooperate now? I sent the kindergartners back to their seats with their parents and began to get the youth into their places around the chancel area.

The youth were snickering and some, a bit high on the beer, were outright laughing at me as I tried to get them arranged to begin their Christmas drama. Finally, they were all seated in their places. The congregation quieted, with even the children and babies seeming to barely breathe as we waited to see what the teens would do in their first ever Christmas Eve program.

The youth sat looking straight at the audience and not speaking at all. I was sure they were not going to cooperate. Some of them looked just plain scared; the others looked belligerent. The stress was getting to all of us. Just as I was going to tell them to come down from the chancel area to make room for the other children's programs, the main character stood and rather flawlessly recited his part. He did not particularly do it well, but he knew it word for word. Each then stood and recited his or her part in turn. The simple little pageant about Jesus' birth was over in less than ten minutes. It was not very sophisticated in light of the age of these youth.

The congregation, however, sensed the urgent need to reward them for their effort to share in the worship that Christmas Eve. They jumped to their feet and cheered and applauded as the youth moved toward the back of the church.

"What happened to you guys?" I asked them later that evening. "Aw heck," one young woman told me, "we didn't really think you cared if we came tonight or not. If Ken hadn't come roaring down main street acting like a crazy guy rounding us up and telling us how important it was for us to come, you'd have never seen any of us again. See you next week."

For the remainder of my three years serving that church, most of the youth did not miss a Sunday. Did they all turn their lives around and never get in trouble again? Oh, no. I visited one of the young women in the psychiatric ward more than once after suicide attempts. Two of the boys were eventually committed to the Juvenile Detention Center.

On one trip to a youth rally, we stopped to have hamburgers; and some of the youth stole all the salt and pepper shakers, napkins, and straws. We had to drive two miles back so they could personally return the stolen property to the restaurant manager. When Ken took several of the boys to a district youth rally, they unscrewed all the chairs in the row in front of them, so that when the other youth came to sit down, the chairs fell apart.

No, they did not all become filled with piety. But I know that once a week, for three years, these young people were in church, hearing the Bible read and the gospel message preached. God will have to take it from there in each of their future lives. They certainly taught me a great deal about God's grace, however.

Paul explains the reason for God's graceful act in the coming of the light of Christ: "That he might redeem us from all iniquity and purify for himself a people of his own who are zealous for good deeds" (2:14). On this last Christmas of the century and the millennium, these verses remind us that God has done everything for just one reason—that we might live in relationship to God throughout our whole lives. God has given us a way to live in piety with him, as well as a way to find our way back to God if somehow we have gotten off the right path.

Who in your church needs to know what it means to be a follower of Jesus Christ?

Who around you needs to know about the wonderful mercy of God's grace?

How can you share the light of the gospel in deeds or spirit?

What have you done this week to strengthen your piety and relationship with God?

What can you do during this next year? this next century?

TIDINGS OF THE BIRTH OF JESUS
Luke 2:1-20

So the long-awaited night comes, and we move from the anticipation of the Advent season into the remembrance of the fulfillment of Christmas Day.

Every Christmas Eve service seems to center around the words of Luke 2:1-20. Perhaps many persons, if asked to do so, could recite most of these well-known words or at least tell the story in great detail: "In those days a decree went out from Caesar Augustus."

Immediately, when we hear these words, we move our thoughts back to another time, another place. We see the bustling town of Bethlehem, full of visitors and merchants and military folks. Then we envision a small donkey and a pregnant young woman accompanied by an older man. The young woman is tired from her long journey.

For a moment, as we listen to the words, we see the innkeeper who at least lets the weary couple go into the stable to rest for the night. Then quickly our minds move to a starry night and fields full of sheep and shepherds overcome by myriads of angelic messengers singing about the tiny newborn baby in the manger.

Finally, we hear about Mary's response of holding all these wonderful memories deep in her heart (2:19). As you come to this Christmas, think once again of the comfort, hope, truth, light, and joy that you find in these verses.

Gaze at the manger scene in your mind. Who is there? A young maiden, perhaps fourteen or fifteen years old, is looking at her firstborn son. She is far from home and had no choice but to give birth in a stable full of animals. An angel has told her that her son is special and that he is the one Isaiah spoke of so long ago: "For a child has been born for us. . . . Authority rests upon his shoulders; and he is named Wonderful Counselor, Mighty God, Everlasting Father, Prince of Peace" (9:6). Mary is a humble Jewish girl, but she will host shepherds and angels and kings who will come to visit her child.

What feelings might you see reflected in Mary's eyes in that manger scene? Wonder? Awe? Fear? Hopefulness? Love? Joy?

Then there is Joseph. He is probably older and more mature than Mary. He did not believe what Mary told him about her child at first. Then God sent an angel to confirm that what Mary said was true. The Holy Spirit had come upon her, and she had conceived this special child. Joseph may still be wondering how this all happened and may be silently praying he has done what he was supposed to do for his wife Mary and the Child.

Perhaps Joseph is also fearful about his role to come in the life of the baby lying in the manger before him. For Joseph, as a Jewish man, is probably familiar with Isaiah 9:7: "His authority shall grow continually, and there shall be endless peace for the throne of David and his kingdom."

Looking into that manger in your mind, what are you thinking about this Christmas? Perhaps you wonder how it really was for Joseph and Mary. Perhaps you would like to have actually seen this fully God/fully human infant so that your faith might be stronger. Perhaps you are simply remembering that the manger is now full. Jesus, the Light, whom we have been waiting for, has arrived. Not in the mighty armor of a warrior but in the fragile, lovely, soft, breakable skin of a newborn baby.

Why do we read Luke 2:1-20 over and over again? It is, after all, the same old story. Nothing new seems to be there. Yet that is precisely the reason we read it again and again. It is the same old story; but since the story comes from the inspiration of God, it is always new. Always fresh. Always the "tidings of joy" that we as Christians are called to share. We cannot share the gospel, however, until we fully accept it ourselves.

> *We cannot share the gospel until we fully accept it ourselves.*

Who of us cannot be touched when we hear the story and the wondrous words of the angelic messengers: "Glory to God in the highest heaven, and on earth peace among those whom he favors!" (2:14). Yet, sadly, on every Christmas many persons are not remembering Jesus Christ and the day he was wrapped in flesh and began to live among us. Many persons still do not know the joy of comfort and hope that Jesus brought when he brought the light to each of us. Many persons have

TIDINGS OF JOY—THE LIGHT IS HERE!

never basked in the light that shines on the dark places in our personal human nature and enriches them—changes them—makes us better persons than we were before.

Sometimes we go to God and ask why God is not doing something about this situation. Why isn't God telling these folks what they need to hear? Why isn't God doing anything about this problem? And, softly, but clearly, we can hear God's reply—"But I have done something. That's why I created you."

What tidings of joy would you like to share with someone in order to make those tidings come alive and real for yourself?

How might you share those tidings of joy with someone who is unchurched or who cannot come to worship because of ill health?

How might you share those tidings of joy with your family?

CONCLUSION

In our lectionary passages we find the complete message of the coming of the Light that can bring us tidings of joy throughout the coming year and in the next millennium. The Light is coming, Isaiah shouted down through the centuries: "For a child has been born to us." Luke reports that while Mary and Joseph were in Bethlehem, "she gave birth to her firstborn son," the fulfillment of Isaiah's prophecy of the Light. Then Paul confirms in the Letter to Titus the promise of the Light's return. In the meantime, let us share the tidings of joy.

Meet the Writer

Mary E. McQueen is pastor of First United Methodist Church, Fullerton, Nebraska. A graduate of Dakota State University and North American Baptist Seminary, she is an ordained elder in the Nebraska Annual Conference. Mary has also served as associate pastor of Centenary United Methodist Church in southeastern Nebraska.

Mary and her husband, Ken, are part of a clergy couple who followed the call to the full-time ministry later in life. Prior to entering seminary, they worked together as owner-operators of five businesses and were lay speakers for the Dakota Annual Conference. The McQueens have spent several years in prison ministries; and Mary has developed a curriculum for a Living Lord's Supper that can be presented in a penitentiary setting, requiring no sets or costumes or lines to learn. The couple has raised five children.

Mary has also been active in cross cultural ecumenical efforts, teaching childbirth preparation and parenting classes, and as an advocate for abused women and children. She has developed curriculum and dramas used in family camps and confirmation camps in the Dakota and Nebraska Annual Conference.